This book belongs to

The Book Of Shadowboxes

Ω

Published by
PEACHTREE PUBLISHERS, LTD.
1700 Chattahoochee Avenue
Atlanta, Georgia 30318-2112

www.peachtree-online.com

Manufactured in Hong Kong
10 9 8 7

Written and illustrated by Laura L. Seeley

Library of Congress Cataloging-in-Publication Data

Seeley, Laura L., 1958–
    The book of shadowboxes.

    Summary: Introduces the letters of the alphabet with a verse for
each letter accompanied by illustrations of appropriate people, objects,
and animals shown inside a shadowbox.
            1. Alphabet rhymes.   2. Children's poetry, American.
[1. Alphabet]   I. Title.
PS3569.E343B6   1989   811'.54   [E]   89-3804
ISBN 0-934601-65-8 Hardcover
ISBN 1-56145-072-3 Trade paperback

The Book Of Shadowboxes

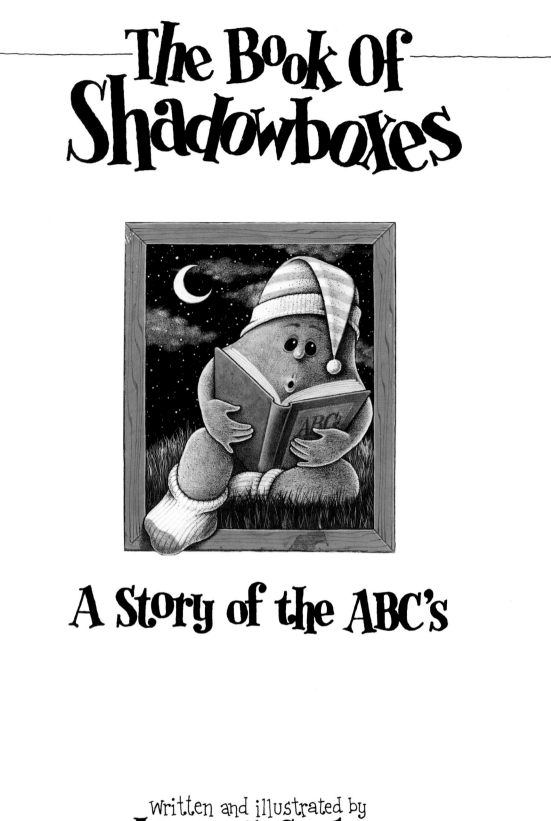

A Story of the ABC's

written and illustrated by
Laura L. Seeley

PEACHTREE PUBLISHERS
ATLANTA

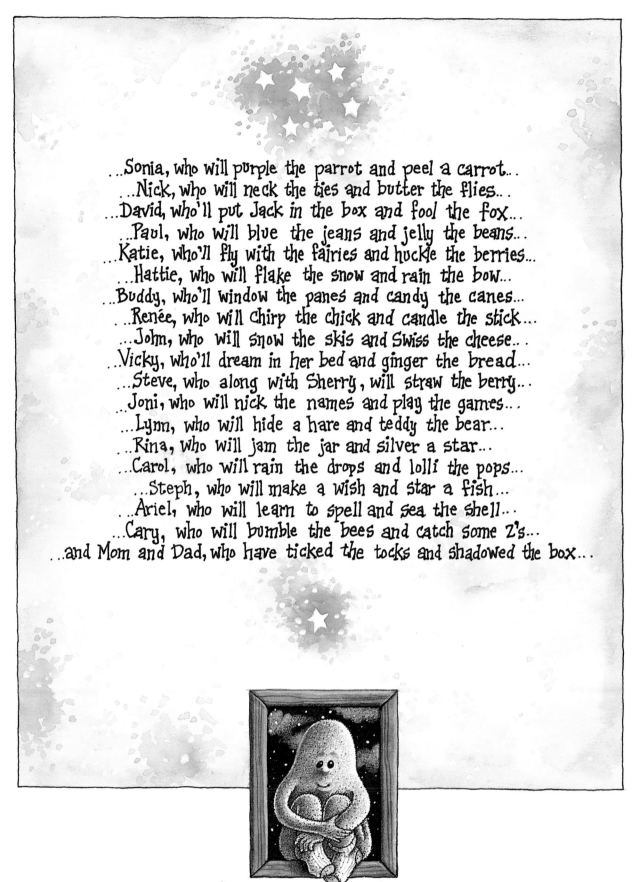

...Sonia, who will purple the parrot and peel a carrot...
...Nick, who will neck the ties and butter the flies...
...David, who'll put Jack in the box and fool the fox...
...Paul, who will blue the jeans and jelly the beans...
...Katie, who'll fly with the fairies and huckle the berries...
...Hattie, who will flake the snow and rain the bow...
...Buddy, who'll window the panes and candy the canes...
...Renée, who will chirp the chick and candle the stick...
...John, who will snow the skis and Swiss the cheese...
...Vicky, who'll dream in her bed and ginger the bread...
...Steve, who along with Sherry, will straw the berry...
...Joni, who will nick the names and play the games...
...Lynn, who will hide a hare and teddy the bear...
...Rina, who will jam the jar and silver a star...
...Carol, who will rain the drops and lolli the pops...
...Steph, who will make a wish and star a fish...
...Ariel, who will learn to spell and sea the shell...
...Cary, who will bumble the bees and catch some Z's...
...and Mom and Dad, who have ticked the tocks and shadowed the box...

Family folks and a few special friends
Are to whom this sincere dedication extends.

The Book Of Shadowboxes

"My name is Shadow,
    And I'll take you places
Through alphabet boxes
    With smiling faces.

Each letter greets you
    With pictures and rhyme,
Then I'll ask you to spot
    Something extra- of mine!

Look a bit harder
    To find even more,
And discover a world of things
    When you explore..."

"The end of this book holds the answers you seek... but pick them out first before taking a peek!"

A is for apple,
   But that's nothing new,
There are apricots, also
   And alphabet stew.

Angels and airplanes
   That sail away,
And a couple of acorns
   On a brisk autumn day.

"CAN YOU FIND MY GREEN APPLE?"

Bananas and butterflies
Both start with B's,
And little blue bubbles
That bounce in the breeze.

A big batch of bunny heads
Row after row,
And a bunch of balloons
With a brown bear below.

"WHERE IS MY BRASS BUGLE?"

Clouds and a castle
Begin with a C,
Some cinnamon circles
And a cat in a tree.

A candy cane crowd
And a couple of clowns,
Then some colorful crayons
Capped with little gold crowns.

"WHERE ARE MY CHOCOLATE CHIP COOKIES?"

D is for dominoes,
    Doughnuts and dice,
Dollies with dimples
    In dresses so nice.

Dragonflies dancing
    With daffodil heads,
And doggies like Doc
    Sharing dreams in our beds.

"CAN YOU FIND MY DRUM?"

Enjoy a few **e**asy things
Using an **E**,
With your **e**ars you can hear
And your **e**yes you can s**ee**.

Find **e**ight **E**nglish **e**lves
And a small **E**skimo,
With the **e**ggs, all **e**leven
And an **e**l**e**phant show.

"WILL YOU LOOK FOR MY **E**IGHTEEN **E**NVELOPES?"

F will find frankfurts
And flowery places,
Five-year-old friends
Who have freckly faces.

Some fun-loving fairies
Who flicker and fly,
And fat little fish
Who go floating on by.

"CAN YOU FIND MY FORK?"

G has a gift—
   It goes three different ways,
The gingerbread men
   Will sound soft, like the J's.

Green grapes will sound hard,
   Like ghost and gumball,
But the gnome has a G
   That you don't hear at all.

"WHERE DID I PUT MY GUITAR?"

H begins hamburgers,
 Hollies and hair,
A house in the hills
 And a hat that you wear.

A hare in the huckleberries
 Hidden away,
And Halloween night
 When the hobgoblins play.

"Where is my harp?"

I is for icecubes
        And icecream cones, too,
And irises, flowers
        Of indigo blue.

An inchworm that rides
        On an ivory snowflake,
And an island that sits
        By itself in the lake.

"WHERE DID I PUT MY IRON?"

Join J with a jam jug
And jellybeans, too,
A joyful old joker
And a jay that is blue.

Some jigsaw pieces
That will fit right in,
And a jack o' lantern
With a jolly big grin.

"CAN YOU FIND MY JACK-IN-THE-BOX?"

K begins kids,
Kangaroos and keys,
But K Keeps quiet
For knitting and knees.

There's Kiki the kitten
Who's so hard to find,
And a kooky old koala,
The king of his kind.

"WHERE IS MY KETTLE?"

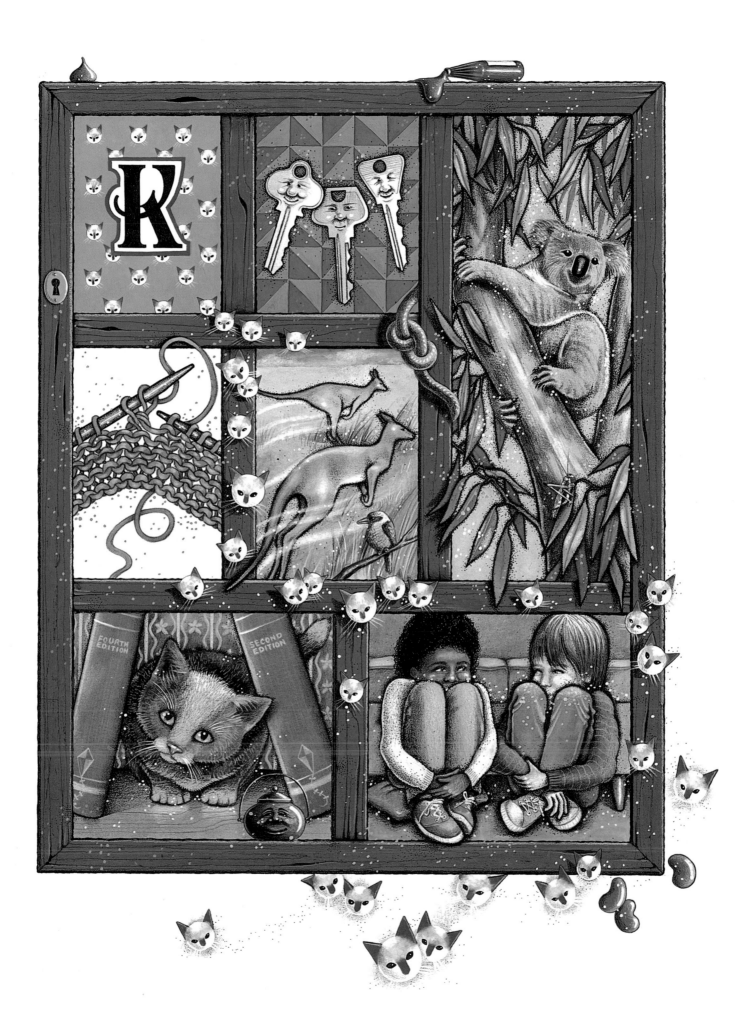

A leaf and a ladybug
Start with an L,
Like lemons and limes
And letters that spell.

A lion named Leo
With a loud lazy yawn,
And laughing lollipops
You can lick 'til they're gone.

"WILL YOU LOOK FOR MY LAMP?"

M begins mushrooms
   And more words like these...
Monkey and moon,
     Macaroni-and-cheese.

Mountains and a mermaid
   Who meet by the sea,
And marigolds under
   A marshmallow tree.

"WHERE IS MY MASK?"

N is for neckties
And nicknames and never,
And numbers for counting
That go on forever.

A noise in the nighttime
When nightcreatures creep,
And nasty old nightmares
That nag in your sleep.

"WHERE DID I PUT MY NOTEBOOK?"

Oodles of oysters
Will open with O,
And their octopus friend
In the ocean below.

Oval-shaped olives
And an orangy crew,
With a clever old owl
Who calls out "Hoo-Hoo!"

"WHERE IS MY OATMEAL?"

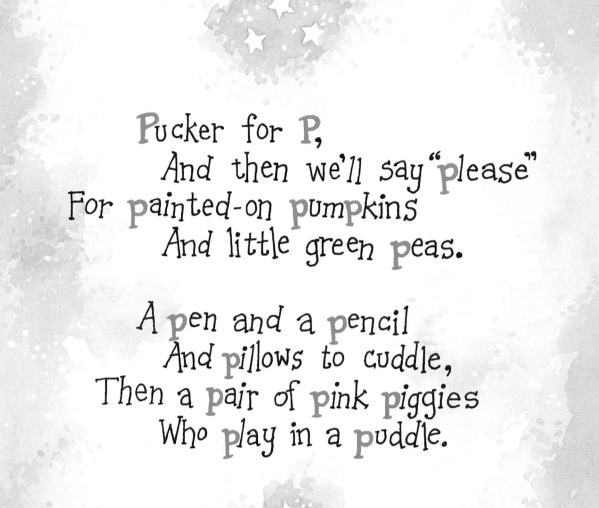

Pucker for P,
  And then we'll say "please"
For painted-on pumpkins
  And little green peas.

A pen and a pencil
  And pillows to cuddle,
Then a pair of pink piggies
  Who play in a puddle.

"Can you find my pet puppy?"

It's quite a bit queer
When it comes to the Q,
The letter that follows
Is always a U.

Like questions, quintuplets,
Quack, quarter and queens,
And a quilt made of quails
For quiet-time scenes.

"WHERE DID I PUT MY QUOTATION MARKS?"

R begins words
    Such as ribbon and rose,
And the wintertime red
    On your round cheeks and nose.

A rainbow beyond
    All the rows of raindrops,
And a running raccoon
    On the rising rooftops.

"WILL YOU LOOK FOR MY ROCKING HORSE?"

S stands for stars
And strawberry strands,
Seashells and starfish
On summertime sands.

Sailboats and sunshine
And a square of Swiss cheese,
A smile on Saturn
And a snowman on skis.

"WHERE IS MY SANDWICH?"

T is for twins
  And telling the time,
Two teddybears
  And a tree you can climb.

Ten little tulips
  That thrive near the road,
And a turtle who talks
  To a tiny tree toad.

"WHERE IS MY TOY TRUMPET?"

Some unusual undershirts
Start with a U,
An upside-down cake
And a unicorn, too.

An umbrella held upward
   To catch the raindrops,
With us underneath it
   Until the rain stops.

"Can you find my ukulele?"

This verse begins
As we visit the V's,
A violin, some veggies
And more words like these...

A vase full of violets
And velvet valentines,
Then to voice a bit more,
Some very long vines.

"WHERE ARE MY VITAMINS?"

W starts watermelons
And wicked old witch,
A black widow weaving
Her web stitch by stitch.

A wizard whirling wind
With his wand in a cave,
And a white whale riding
A watery wave.

"Can you find my wishbone?"

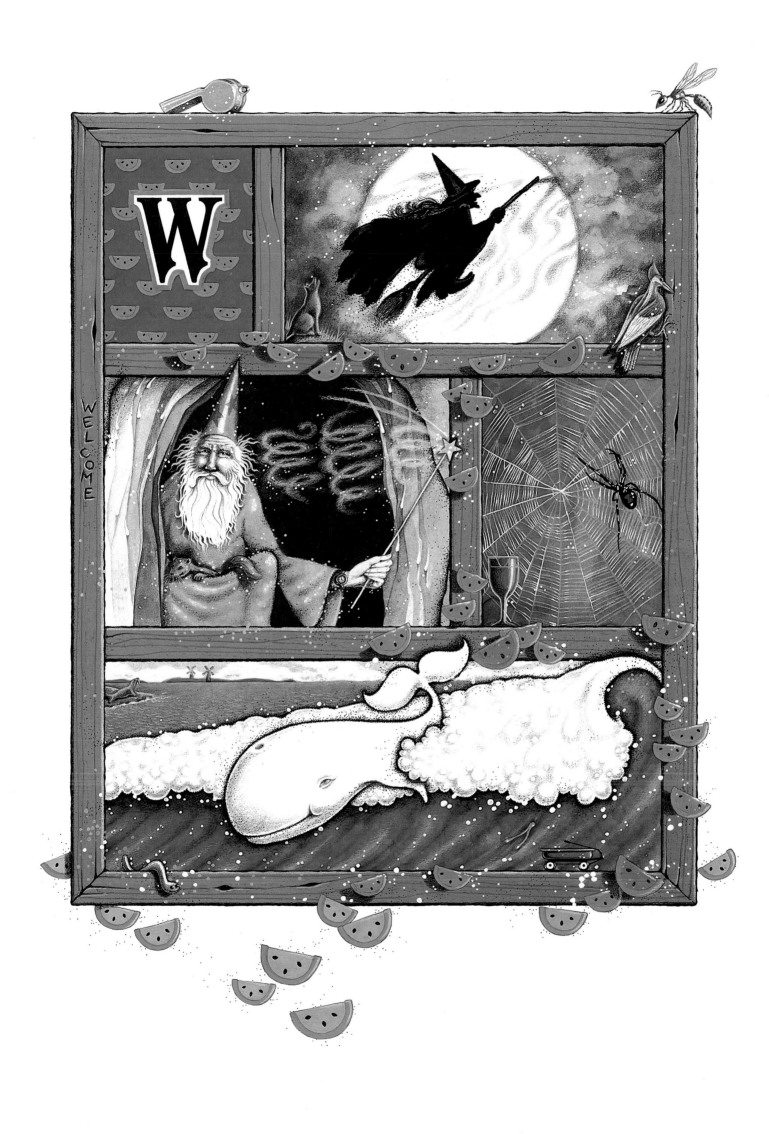

X doesn't start
    Many words, just a few,
But it's mixed in with taxi
    And chickenpox, too.

Six waxen candles
    And Dixie the fox,
Then sixty-six letters
    In the next mailbox.

"Where did I put my saxophone?"

Yes, this is Y,
　　Which starts yardstick and yak,
And the yolks you will find
　　Inside eggs when they crack.

Yarnballs of yellow
　　Becoming unwound,
And your own little yoyos
　　That spin 'round and 'round.

"WHERE DID I PUT MY YOGURT?"

A little boy Zach
Catches zillions of Z's,
There's a zipper that zigzags
And more words like these...

A zebra named Ziggy
Who lives in a zoo,
And some zany old zeroes
With nothing to do.

"Would you like to catch some Z's with me?"

Some things
You might identify...

In case they may
Have missed your eye...

A

~an apparently green apple~
~an avocado~
~an ancient anchor~
~an appetizing artichoke~
~an ace~
~an amiable armadillo~
~an attentive alligator~
~five active ants~
~an anxious anteater~
~an assembly of arches~

B

~a bandaged boo boo~
~a bow tie~
~a black beetle-bug~
~a beak~
~a background of bricks~
~a brand-new belt~
~blue bells~
~a buzzing bumblebee~
~a brass bugle~
~a beautiful baby bluebird~
~a book~
~a baseball bat~
~buttons~
~a bronze belt buckle~
~a baseball~
~a branch of blueberries~
~a bristled broom~
~a basket of bread~

C

~a coffee cup~
~a chirping chick~
~a cupcake~
~a clock~
~countable corners~
~craggy cliffs~
~chocolate chip cookies~
~a cruising cricket~
~a camel~
~a chewing chipmunk~
~a cherry~
~a crawling caterpillar~
~a cozy countryside~
~a candle~
~crunchy carrots~
~a creek~
~a crow~
~a canoe~
~corn on the cob~
~a cow and her cute calf~
~a clover~
~a city~

D

~a dinosaur dragon~
~dazzling diamonds~
~a drum~
~a dappled dalmatian~
~double darts~
~a diving dolphin~
~daisies~
~a dusty dictionary~
~ducks~
~drumsticks~
~a daddy longlegs~

E

~an emerald egg~
~exactly eighteen envelopes~
~eyeglasses~
~evergreens in the evening~
~an eggplant you can eat~
~elbows~
~an extremely edible eclair~
~eyebrows~
~an earring~
~an example of an eagle~
~an egret~

F

~four feathers~
~a furry fox~
~a football~
~a fancy flamingo~
~a feisty fly~
~a family of fruit~
~fins~
~fluttering fingers~
~a flowing flag~
~feet~
~a flock of footprints~
~a fence~
~a fallen fork~
~flavorful frenchfries~
~fresh ferns~
~a frisky frog~
~a field~

G

~a golden goose~
~a great big grasshopper~
~gripping gloves~
~a genuine giraffe~
~a gorilla~
~a gentle gerbil~
~a gold goblet~
~goggles~
~a goofy grapefruit~
~glasses~
~a glossy guitar~
~green glimmering grass~
~a group of guppies~
~a gray gumball~

H

~a happy hippo~
~hedges~
~a heavy hog~
~a hiding hyena~
~a hose~
~a hawk~
~hearts~
~a herd of horses~
~a harp~
~handwriting~
~a homemade hotdog~
~a hole~
~a horseshoe~
~a hoe~
~a horn~
~a hammer~
~a hazy horizon~
~H_2O~

I

~an igloo~
~india ink~
~icicles~
~an iron~
~identical iceskates~
~an iguana~
~an intelligent imp~
~ivy~

J

~a jackrabbit that jumps~
~jeans~
~a juggler~
~a junior jack-in-the-box~
~a jaguar~
~jumbo jets~
~a jumbled jungle~
~a jackal~
~a jade jar~

K

~a keen kookaburra~
~kites~
~knuckles~
~a kicking katydid~
~a knot~
~ketchup~
~kidney beans~
~a kettle~
~a keyhole~
~khaki pants~
~a kiss~

L

~a lucky, laughing leprechaun~
~a little lizard~
~a ladle~
~a lighted lamp~
~a lock~
~a large lobster~
~a lovable lamb~
~legs~
~limas on the left~
~a long ladder~
~a lively leopard~
~lightning~

M
~a Mischievous Mouse~
~a Match~
~Magic Marbles~
~a Moose~
~Matching Mittens~
~a Mug~
~Merry Musical Notes~
~a Moth~
~a Mysterious Mask~
~a Moustache~
~Marvelous Muffins~
~a Maple Leaf~
~a Miniature Mallet~

N
~Nine Nails~
~a Napping Nose~
~a Nestled Nest~
~Nuts to Nibble On~
~a Neat Notebook~
~a Newspaper~
~Nostrils~
~a Narrow Needle~
~a Net~
~a New Nickel~

O
~Organized Octagons~
~an Ostrich~
~Ordinary Onions~
~Obscure Ornaments~
~an Opal~
~an Opossum Looking Things Over~
~an Otter~
~Oars~
~an Obviously White Owl~
~Oatmeal~

P
~Pretty Pearls~
~a Parade of Pawprints~
~a Pipe~
~a Pattern of Plaid Print~
~a Pretzel on Paper~
~Paint~
~a Purple Parrot~
~a Pie~
~a Plump Peach~
~a Paintbrush~
~Peaceful Palms~
~Perky Penguins~
~a Pet Puppy~
~a Pudgy Panda~
~a Piece of Pizza with Pepperoni~
~a Plug~
~a Perfect Pear~
~a Peeping Pelican~

Q
~a Quivering Question Mark~
~Quadruplets~
~Quotation Marks~
~a Quill~
~Quarrels (Windowpanes)~
~Quicksand~
"Quiz, Quality, Quick, Quart,
Quench, Quit, Quiver,"

R
~a Rushing, Rippling, Rambling River~
~a Rascally Rat~
~a Road~
~a Regular Rolling Pin~
~a Rare Rhino~
~Rocks~
~a Rustic Rocking Horse~
~a Routinely Used Ruler~
~Rays~
~a Resting Robin~
~Rectangles~
~a Rake~
~a Rapidly Romping Rabbit~
~Ripe Raisins~
~a Rickety Rocking Chair~

S
~Seven Silver Stars~
~a Scarf~
~a Sheep to Shear~
~a Sneaker~
~a Small Seahorse~
~The Sky~
~Shadows~
~a Slippery Snake~
~a Sneaky Skunk~
~a Shovel~
~Sharp Scissors~
~Soaring Seagulls~
~Some Straight Stripes~
~a Stork~
~a Slinky Squirrel~
~a Smooth Sunbathing Seal~
~a Sandwich~
~a Suave Swan~
~The Salty, Sparkling Sea~
~Six Spiders~
~a Spoon~
~a Steamship~

T
~Three Thimbles~
~Twelve Tadpoles~
~a Tall Trunk~
~Triangles~
~a Toy Trumpet~
~Tails~
~a Trio of Tomatoes~
~a Traveling Train~
~a Tunnel~
~a Thumb Tack~
~Toes~
~Two Tickets~
~a Truck~
~a Teepee~
~a Tame Toucan~
~a Tough Tiger~
~Tongues~
~a "Tick-Tock"~
~a Toothbrush~

U
~an Urn~
~an Unwavering Unicycle~
~a Ukulele~
~an Unkempt Urchin~
~The Union Jack~
~an Upside-Down Umbrella~
~Useful Utensils~
~Uncle Sam in His Uniform~

V
~Valuable Versatile Vowels~
~a Vane~
~a Violent Volcano~
~a Very Vulnerable Village~
~a Fallen Violet~
~a Voracious Vulture~
~a Van~
~a Variety of Vitamins~
~a View of a Valley~
~a Vent~
~a Vile Vampire~

W
~a Wandering Worm~
~Wings~
~a Watchful Walrus~
~Whispering Windmills~
~Wet Walls~
~a Whistle~
~Wispy Whiskers~
~Wonderful Wine~
~a Wee Wagon~
~a Wasp~
~a Worthwhile Wishbone~
~a Wacky Woodpecker~
~Wood~
~a Weasel~
~Working Wheels~
~a Wristwatch~
~a Wild, Wailing Wolf~
~a Word~

X
~an Extra Red X~
~an Exquisite Saxophone~
~an Extraordinary Ox~
~an Axe~
~Six Excited Pixies~
~a Box~
~an Extremely Expensive Tuxedo~

Y
~Yuccas~
~a Yacht~
~Yams~
~Yummy Yogurt~
~a Yawn~
~a Young, Yodeling Yeti~

Z
~a Zeppelin~
~a Zebu~
~Zingy Zinnias~
~Zucchinis~
"Zap, Zone, Zip Code, Zodiac,
Zoom, Zinc, Zest"

One last note...

"We've come to the end
Of this ABC rhyme,
I hope you had fun,
And I'll see you next time."

Your friend,
Shadow